Original title:
Tropical Breeze, Endless Seas

Copyright © 2025 Creative Arts Management OÜ
All rights reserved.

Author: Adrian Caldwell
ISBN HARDBACK: 978-1-80581-631-7
ISBN PAPERBACK: 978-1-80581-158-9
ISBN EBOOK: 978-1-80581-631-7

The Last Light Over Water's Edge

Sunset dances, a silly sight,
Flipping fish jump with pure delight.
A crab in a hat waves goodbye,
Yelling, 'Don't let the seagulls fly!'

As shadows stretch, we laugh and play,
A rogue wave splashes, calls it a day.
The sun winks as it sinks so low,
'Next round's on me!' yells a friendly doe.

Faint Laughter in the Sea Mist

In the fog, whispers tickle the air,
Mermaids giggle, flipping their hair.
A fish tries on a sailor's hat,
Says, 'Look at me, I'm so very fat!'

A dolphin complains, 'I've lost my way,'
While surfers dance on the waves at play.
Shells chuckle as the tide pulls them near,
Whispering secrets only they can hear.

The Feathered Friends of Paradise

Parrots squawk with gossip galore,
'Who wore that last week? It's such a bore!'
Flamingos strut with a clumsy flair,
Tryna impress with one-legged air!

'Fruity drinks!' shrieks an audacious gull,
While pelicans dive with a big ol' hull.
Seagulls' pranks make everyone laugh,
Trading breadcrumbs for a photograph!

Journals of Journeys Unknown

Maps are scribbled with chocolate stains,
Guiding us to puddles of rain.
Crucial notes, 'Watch out for the crab,'
Who steals our chips with a sneaky grab!

Tides flip pages, wind adds the flair,
A parrot reads what's caught in the air.
The journey's goofy, laughter's our guide,
With tales of mischief on this wild ride.

Horizons of Blue and Gold

The sun slipped down with a wink,
The waves laughed and started to stink.
Seagulls squawked with a silly shout,
Chasing crabs that were full of doubt.

Bright kites tangled up in the air,
Kids running wildly without a care.
Sandcastles fell with a soft thud,
While dogs played catch with a muddy dud.

Palm Shadows Under the Moon

Coconuts danced on a breeze so bright,
As dreamers munched on snacks at night.
Laughter echoed through gentle trees,
While salsa steps brought everyone to their knees.

A limbo stick grew tired and aged,
As folks gave it a try, quite enraged.
With each bend more giggles erupted,
That stick now dreams it's been abducted!

Secrets of the Coral Depths

Fish in bow ties swim by with ease,
While clams gossip, sharing their tease.
An octopus juggles, looking quite sly,
As crabs debate who'll win the pie.

A newt wore goggles, much to his cheer,
Declaring the water was far too clear.
With each splash, a bright bubble burst,
Leaving behind tales of underwater firsts.

Driftwood Dreams on Shimmering Shores

Driftwood lounged, acting quite cool,
While seagulls squabbled over a rule.
The tides took a nap, the sand gave a yawn,
As beach balls rolled on until dawn.

A crab in shades posed for a pic,
With a smile so wide, it was quite the trick.
Flip-flops danced in the warming sun,
As laughter reminded all it was fun!

Caressing the Quiet Sands

The crabs hold a meeting, quite serious and grand,
In tiny tuxedos, they scuttle on sand.
With a whispered debate on who's fastest in race,
While seagulls circle, laughing wide in their space.

A starfish named Fred thinks he's quite the big shot,
Says, "I'm the best rug, so please let me be caught!"
But when the tide rolls in, he just floats away,
Crab parties forgotten, like the end of a play.

Fables of Fins and Flukes

The fish share a tale of a bold little minnow,
Who danced with a dolphin named delicate Jimeno.
"I flipped and I flopped, quite the sight, I must say!"
Chimed Jimeno, who splashed in a dramatic display.

But a shark nearby, with a wink and a grin,
Said, "Dance all you want, when the music's within!"
So under the waves, they swam and they twirled,
In a watery world, where laughter unfurled.

Where the Pelicans Play

The pelicans gather to gossip and tease,
"Did you see that fish? He was trying to freeze!"
With a flap and a flap, they dive down for a snack,
But their aim's so off, they forget to come back.

One fell from the sky, did a cartwheel so neat,
Landed smack on a turtle, who now can't find his feet!
With a wink and a smile, they all join the fun,
Chasing their shadows 'til the day is all done.

Glistening Shores at Twilight

As the sun bids adieu, in a glow of delight,
Crabs dance in shadows, their claws taking flight.
The shells have a party, all colors and shapes,
With conch shells as guest stars, doing funny shakes.

A seagull in shades says "Let's boogie tonight!"
While sandcastles whisper and follow the light.
The waves crash in laughter, they roll with a cheer,
As evening draws near, all worries disappear.

Sunsets that Kiss the Water

The sun slips low, a slippery fish,
People chuckle, make a big wish.
With shades on, they squint and giggle,
As colors swirl, and shadows wiggle.

A crab scuttles, quick as a thought,
Stealing fries, what a sly plot!
Laughter erupts, as drinks are spilled,
The ocean's charm, our hearts it thrilled.

Windswept Shores and Sandy Tales

Seagulls squawk, they steal our fries,
While sunscreen jugs turn into pies.
Kids build castles, as waves break down,
Until it's a moat that wears a crown.

Footprints wander in paths of glee,
Paddles flip like they're chasing a bee.
A joke is tossed like a beach ball high,
Splash! A laugh, and wet clothes dry.

The Lure of Distant Islands

Maps with X's, treasures untold,
Like pirates they claim, not very bold.
A parrot squawks, "Arr matey, share!"
While sunburnt friends lounge without a care.

Sipping coconuts, feeling so grand,
Chasing dreams on a sun-kissed sand.
Then someone yells, "Look, a whale!"
Turns out it's just a rubber sale.

Caress of the Trade Winds

Winds whistle tunes, like a saxophone,
While beach towels dance, quite out of tone.
Fins and goggles, where did they go?
Oh wait, a dog joined the water show!

With kites in flight, it's a comical sight,
Looping and swirling in pure delight.
The breeze tickles, we all start to sneeze,
Laughing together with sand in our knees.

Breezes Carrying Secrets of the Depth

The wind confides in waves so grand,
Gossip drifts to shores of sand.
Fish in shades of lime and teal,
Swim in circles, what a deal!

Seagulls flapping, squawking loud,
Join the fish; they're part of the crowd.
"Who stole my crab?" one bird cries out,
As the waves just laugh and pout.

Jellyfish dance with a jiggly wiggle,
While whales do a twist with a playful giggle.
The ocean has tales that'll make you grin,
Where surfboards chat and dolphins spin!

Every splash is a secret shared,
In this watery world, all is bared.
With a wink from the shells, they declare,
The ocean's life is beyond compare!

Tides that Whisper Timeless Truths

The waves roll in with a chuckle and sigh,
"Did you hear the tide's joke? Oh my!"
Sandcastles topple, but don't shed a tear,
The sea's got laughs waiting right here.

Ebb and flow with a smile, they tease,
"Did the crab just wear my car keys?"
Clams laugh softly, their faces aglow,
As kelp swings by, putting on a show.

Sailboats prance on the frothy peaks,
As friendly dolphins swim and sneak.
"Why did the fish blush?" one waves pokes,
"Because it saw the net of the folks!"

The shoreline giggles, sea-foam ticks,
With crabby punchlines and fishy tricks.
In every ripple, a story's unfurled,
Of laughter and joy in this splashy world!

Beneath the Sun-Kissed Skies

Sunshine tickles the ocean's face,
While crabs dance about in a comical race.
Flip-flops flop as beachgoers dash,
A giant wave gives them all a splash!

"Why build a castle?" a child once asked,
"It's simpler to surf and have fun masked!"
With sunscreen smears and hats cocked askew,
Seagulls swoop down, in search of a brew.

At high noon, when the laughter's loud,
Sand angels flourish, like a pastel cloud.
Surfboards tell tales of wipeouts and thrills,
While sunburnt noses declare their chills.

Under bright skies, a fiesta of cheer,
With sunflowers laughing, oh so near.
This playful paradise of bowls and seas,
Creates memories boundless, like the breeze!

The Call of the Distant Lighthouse

A lighthouse stands with a silly grin,
It calls out loudly, "Come take a spin!"
But on the rocks, I trip and flop,
With every wave, I dance and hop.

The seagulls laugh, they jest and tease,
While I'm stuck shouting, "Where's my cheese?"
The tide pulls back like a playful dog,
I splash around like a jumping frog.

Chasing Horizons in Golden Light

I dart along the shore, full speed,
With sunblock smeared, I'm quite the breed.
A flip-flop flies, my hat takes flight,
Chasing horizons from morning to night.

The sun dips low, it gives a wink,
While I stumble over a beach ball, oh think!
But laughter spills like sand from my hand,
As I churn up giggles on this golden land.

Beneath the Palm-Laden Skies

There's shade beneath those leafy crowns,
But watch those coconuts, they drop like clowns!
I dodge and weave, a hilarious dance,
While locals chuckle, giving me a glance.

The parrots squawk in mock delight,
As I trip on roots, oh what a sight!
But every slip just adds to the fun,
Underneath the sky, I'm far from done.

Reflections in Gentle Ripples

The water's smooth, reflects my face,
I smile wide, in this silly race.
But suddenly there's a splash nearby,
A fish jumps up, gives me the eye.

I wave hello, it dives and twirls,
While I splash back, causing giggles and swirls.
Each ripple laughs, it tickles my feet,
In this shiny pond, such joy can't be beat.

Where the Sand Meets the Sky

When the sun laughs and the waves play,
Seagulls steal snacks, what can we say?
Sandcastles crumbling with every tide,
And kids chasing dreams, nowhere to hide.

Flip-flops flapping, they lose their grip,
A tumble here, a sand-filled zip.
Beach balls bouncing, a comical flight,
Oh, the silly dance of pure delight.

Sunburned noses and sandy toes,
Dodging the waves, nobody knows.
With ice cream melting down our hand,
Laughter rings out, oh isn't this grand?

As dusk falls softly, glowsticks in hand,
We twirl and shimmy, so unplanned.
With shadows dancing, the night grows new,
And in the warm glow, we bid adieu.

Reflections in Motion

Waves invite us for a cheeky leap,
But faith's a friend we rarely keep.
Footprints washed away without a care,
While dolphins giggle, we splash everywhere.

Mirrors of water, so slippery sweet,
Trying to stand, we topple our feet.
Sun hats flying, sunblock is smeared,
With laughter that follows, we're endlessly cheered.

The quirky crabs scuttle on by,
They wave their claws like they're shy.
Riding the currents, a whimsical chase,
Who knew a swim could be such a race?

We dance with the shadows upon the sand,
As evening sets in, we still take a stand.
Reflections that sparkle, mishaps galore,
Chasing the tide, who could want more?

Odyssey of the Gentle Current

Floating along on a noodle so bright,
Who knew relaxation could equal such fright?
The fish laugh at us, splashing with joy,
As we paddle like pros, but feel like a toy.

Oar in one hand, a drink in the other,
This balance we've struck? A true shaky brother.
The sun overhead is our biggest fan,
While ducks quack loudly, plotting a plan.

Setting sail for snacks, we drift out of bounds,
In search of coconuts, ignoring the sounds.
Palm fronds above scratch our sun-kissed skin,
In this comedy act, we're destined to win.

Bellying up to the bar of the sea,
We laugh and we trip, all wild and free.
And when the day ends with giggles and cheers,
We promise to return, through laughter and tears.

Surrender to the Sea's Embrace

Caught in the waves, what a wild dance,
Trying to swim, but it's more like a prance.
With floaties on, it's all a grand show,
As we splash and we tumble with nowhere to go.

Seashells collected—what a strange find,
A pirate's treasure or just cleverly designed?
With each silly stumble and graceful fail,
Life's laughter rises like a comical sail.

Beach towels bunched like fortresses made,
In the kingdom of sun, our worries all fade.
A crab wears a crown, a ruler in disguise,
We bow to the sun, in laughter, we rise.

At night we gather, the stars shining bright,
Swapping tales of the day, timeless delight.
With our hearts all aglow, we embrace this spree,
The sea keeps our secrets, just you and me.

Tidepool Tales at Dawn

In the early glow, crabs take a stroll,
Giggling fish play games, fitting into their role.
A starfish claims a rock, stuck like a boss,
While seaweed dances, showing all it's gloss.

Little snails race slow, what a sight to see,
Conch shells gossip, whispering with glee.
A sea cucumber slips, then makes a big splat,
While a curious clam debates where it's at.

Flip-flops flounder, caught in the tide,
Beach balls tumble, rolling like they've died.
Seagulls squawking jokes, they think they're so funny,
While the sun is rising, wearing bright, hot honey.

And as we gather, with buckets and nets,
We chuckle at nature, it's full of odd sets.
The shoreline's alive with silly antics to share,
In the glamour of dawn, we breathe in the flair.

Palette of the Coral Kingdom

In the depths so bright, colors collide,
Fish in tuxedos swirl with the tide.
A shrimp with a bowtie, bold as can be,
Dancing with jellies, oh, what a spree!

Anemones giggle at clumsy old eels,
While parrotfish chuckle, revealing their meals.
With coral so vibrant, it's a sight to behold,
The reef's an art gallery, stories unfold.

Clownfish paint stripes, full of mischief and glee,
Telling tall tales about their best spree.
While a blenny collects bizarre bits of junk,
Declaring that treasure aren't just for the hunk!

With a sprinkle of sea salt, we laugh and we play,
In this magical kingdom, come join the ballet.
Every wave brings a chuckle, in colors so bold,
In the palette of life, fun is pure gold.

Windswept Bliss by the Bay

The seagulls take flight, announcing their dreams,
While a crab draws a map in the sand, or so it seems.
A flip-flop flies off, a daring escape,
Chasing down laughter, what a silly shape!

Kites are a-flutter, tangled in a tree,
While children are rolling in giggles of glee.
A coconut drops, an awful loud thud,
And the beach ball bounces, splashing in mud.

Sunbathers reclining, some with odd hats,
While kids with buckets are chasing the spats.
The whispering waves sing a goofy tune,
Sharing the secrets of the round afternoon.

With banana boat rides and laughter endured,
The bay is our playground, forever assured.
In the windswept embrace, joy is our key,
We'll dance through the frolic, so wild and free.

A Dance of Paper Lanterns

As the sun dips down, lanterns take flight,
Floating like fireflies, embracing the night.
A paper fish flops, laughing as it goes,
Balloons of mischief, ready for all shows!

The crabs put on shoes, waltzing with flair,
While fish play the drums, never a care.
With the moon overhead, casting a glow,
A party of shadows, come join the show!

Everyone twirls with giggles and cheer,
Beneath the bright stars, there's mischief so near.
A lantern oxidizes, oh, dear, what a mess,
Laughing at moments we can't quite impress.

So here's to joy under the starry embrace,
Where lanterns in paper dance with such grace.
With every chuckle, the night sails away,
In this funny adventure, we choose to stay.

The Harmony of Shells and Sand

A crab in a tux, with a dapper stout,
Told a fish with a hat, "We've got to head out!"
They danced on the shore, what a sight to behold,
While the seagulls all laughed and the oysters turned bold.

The sand was their stage, the waves played the tune,
A clam sang a solo, in the light of the moon.
"Here comes the tide!" shouted one with a grin,
And they all ran in circles, with shells on their chin.

When the sun took a nap and the stars danced anew,
A jellyfish joined, with a cape made of blue.
The crowd cheered aloud, as the ripples did clap,
With seaweed confetti, they kicked up a flap.

Then a dolphin jumped high and swirled through the spout,
"Come join us, dear friends!" with a flip and a shout!
So they laughed through the night, as the ocean did sway,
In a hullabaloo, 'neath the warm Milky Way.

Legends Carried by Ocean Waves

A walrus in shades sipped a drink with a grin,
Telling tales of his youth, as he mulled with a fin.
The waves rolled in gossip of pirates long gone,
While crabs took the stage, playing tunes till the dawn.

"Did you hear of the ship that was lost near the reef?"
Asked a seagull who cawed, half in joy and in grief.
With a wink and a nod, the walrus replied,
"I found their old map, but my treasure, I fried!"

As the dolphins all chuckled, sailing high in the air,
A turtle in overalls said, "Let's go on a dare!"
So they raced through the foam, what a sight to behold,
While the fish formed a chorus, "Will you share your gold?"

Riding waves like a rollercoaster crew,
They laughed 'til they cried, the whole ocean's revue.
With legends and laughter, their hearts filled with glee,
On those shimmering shores, they found joyful esprit.

The Color of Dusk in a Tropical Dream

A parrot in pajamas sang tunes on a spree,
While a dolphin wore glasses, as cool as could be.
They danced through the dusk, with a flair and a twist,
With jellyfish grooving, they couldn't resist.

"The sky's turning purple!" a crab raised a claw,
While the sea whispered secrets, a marvelous law.
They painted the horizon with strokes of delight,
While the fish wore their best clothes, all sparkling bright.

"Is that sunset sushi?" the parrot exclaimed,\nWith the
taste of the sea, by the flavors unnamed.
They feasted on laughter, with seaweed for zest,
As they dreamed of new colors, in their oceanic quest.

Then stars popped like popcorn in black velvet skies,
With the moon as their chaperone, shining wise.
Each wave brought a giggle, a splash, and a cheer,
For in this vivid dream, there was nothing to fear!

Embracing the Echo of Seafoam

A sea snail with headphones jammed out on the sand,
While a fish blew a trumpet, taking a stand.
The seafoam was jumping, with rhythm to sway,
As the crabs formed a conga, in a frothy ballet.

"Who knew the beach party could get so surreal?"
Said a clam doing cartwheels, "Now that's quite a deal!"
The sea urchins spun, in their spiky état,
While the waves gave a nod, feeling cool and relaxed.

With each splash they embraced, a giggling delight,
Dancing shadows of night brought a magical sight.
An octopus DJ, spinning tunes like a pro,
With sea cucumbers grooving, the rep still aglow.

The echoes of laughter bounced off every shell,
With that wild beach vibe, they condition for well.
"As the foamy night wraps us, let's twirl and we'll cheer,
For tomorrow the sunrise will bring another tear!"

Horizon's Embrace at Dusk

The sun waves goodbye, what a sight to see,
As my hat takes flight, oh, how it does flee!
Drinks spill like secrets, laughter fills the air,
Dancing like crabs, without a single care.

Flip-flops in hand, we chase after sunset,
But tripped on a shell, oh my, what a threat!
We tumble and giggle, a sandy ballet,
As the sky turns to pink, we choose to stay while we play.

Song of the Driftwood Wanderers

The driftwood sings, oh, what a tune!
It rolls on the shore, under the bright moon.
Seagulls drop jokes from height with great flair,
While we laugh and squawk, like we don't have a care.

A coconut falls, what a silly surprise!
We dodge and we weave, dodging fruity goodbyes!
With a splash and a dash, we're gliding on waves,
Who knew wood could dance, in its own little ways?

Abandonment to the Lapping Waves

The waves tickle toes, oh, what a tease!
I drop my ice cream, in sheer shock and sneeze!
With sunscreen on noses, we frolic and play,
While llamas in flip-flops cheer us on hooray!

Saltwater drips from my squeaky clean chin,
While my buddy's lost shoes are—well, they're sunk in!
We laugh, roll around, like jellyfish glee,
As the tide takes our worries, oh, so carefree!

Solstice Dreams in Sun's Arms

In shades too bright, we lounge like it's fate,
My drink's gone rogue, that's one slippery mate!
A crab scuttles by, with quite the right strut,
I'm convinced he's lost, in this sandy glut.

The sun wraps us tight, in its warm, golden glow,
As we swap silly tales, and put on a show.
How can one sit still, when the fun's at its peak?
Tomorrow's still waiting for more laughs to speak!

Secrets Beneath the Azure Surface

Bubbles dance, fish wear a tie,
Crabs moonwalk as they scuttle by.
A mermaid's lost her favorite shell,
Now she's stuck in a clammy spell.

Jellyfish float in lazy ease,
They throw a party, if you please.
But don't forget the piña coladas,
They'll knock out the best of your balladas.

Seaweed wigs and starfish hats,
Octopus jokes, riddles, and chats.
All the critters laugh out loud,
Making waves, they feel so proud.

So dive down where the secrets spin,
Join the fun as the chaos begins.
Underwater whimsy, who can believe?
Nature's jesters, take off your sleeve.

Radiant Sunset's Call

The sky wears orange, like a clown,
As seagulls dive to snatch a frown.
Sun's slipping down, gives a wink,
Painting the waves with a splash of pink.

Surfers tumble, all flailing grace,
Chasing the waves in a goofy race.
One falls off, yelling, "Catch me, please!"
While others laugh like mischievous bees.

Palm trees sway, dancing in tunes,
Under a circus of evening moons.
Beach balls bounce, flying in cheer,
While sandcastles whisper, "We're still here!"

So let the sunset steal your heart,
Let's toast to laughter, the ocean's art.
With flip-flops off, join this ball,
Beach day mischief, come one, come all!

Voyage of the Crystal Waters

A boat made of noodles, sailing fast,
Fueled by laughter, a cheery blast.
Navigating seas of mystery mist,
With dolphins performing, they can't resist.

Captain's got a rubber ducky crew,
Navigating with a giggle or two.
They sing sea shanties, off-key delight,
Waving to fishes in a splashy fight.

Mermaids cheer with a silly jest,
"Join our dance!" they bubble and jest.
Fishes don their best sparkly suits,
While turtles slow-dance, shaking their boots.

Soride the waves, let whims be your breeze,
While seahorses serve up fresh sea tease.
We'll drift along with waves as our guide,
On this funny voyage, let humor ride!

Harmonies of the Distant Horizon

Seashell melodies drift on the air,
While crabs play duets without a care.
Stars align in a goofy ballet,
Synchronized moves, hey, come out and play!

The sun does its dance, in heels no less,
And waves mock the clouds, causing a mess.
Sea cucumbers hum a soft tune,
Under the glow of a giggling moon.

Look out, a whale's doing the twist,
Incredibly funny, you get the gist.
The ocean stirs with joyous songs,
As jellyfish jive, moving along.

So linger awhile, just follow the beat,
In laughing waters, find your own seat.
With harmonies echoing, let spirits rise,
Together we feast on the ocean's surprise!

Waves of Serenity and Soul

In flip-flops, I chase the tide,
A crab scuttles, I leap aside.
Seagulls squawk, they steal my fries,
While salty winds swirl 'round like spies.

My sunburn's bright, a fiery glow,
I dance with waves, put on a show.
But then my hat flies off, oh dear!
The ocean laughs, I shed a tear.

My drink spills out, a colorful splash,
As I pretend it's all a grand bash.
A dolphin jumps, waves hello,
I wave back, feeling quite the pro.

With sand in shoes and laughs on file,
Each wave brings joy, each splash a smile.
Funny moments with the sun's embrace,
Life's a party, all in good grace.

Lighthouses in the Mist

A beacon shines, it's time to play,
But seagulls keep stealing my buffet.
I trip on shells, oh what a sight,
With laughter echoing into the night.

In the fog, the lights do dance,
I try to impress with a goofy prance.
The keeper winks, he knows my games,
As I star in my own silly claims.

A lighthouse spins, my head does too,
Lost my friends, but I found a shoe.
With sandcastles built, I'm king today,
Joy in the mist, in every way.

The waves crash loud, but I don't care,
I'm here for fun, not for a dare.
With jokes and giggles to share with the crew,
This harbor life's a silly view.

Celestial Rhythms of the Coast

At dawn I dance on sandy floors,
As morning breaks, the ocean roars.
With jellyfish nudging my toes,
It's a wiggly jig, in comical prose.

Stars wave bye, as the sun comes near,
I try to surf, but scream in fear.
A board goes flying, a wild ride,
The ocean's chuckle, my slip and slide.

With clams that sing and shells that laugh,
I join the chorus, it's my gaff.
The waves keep clapping, what a fate,
I joke with crabs, they snicker, wait!

Each splash a drum, a song to sing,
I'm the mermaid of this funny fling.
As twilight falls, the fun won't cease,
With laughter echoing, blissful peace.

The Call of the Siren's Sea

A siren sings from a rock quite grand,
But it's just my friend with a rubber band.
She laughs at my float, bright pink and round,
In the splash zone, together we're bound.

Mysterious depths and silly whims,
I splash and twirl, as the sunlight dims.
But then a wave swallows my snack,
Just me and fish, oh what a flak!

Tails of fish, with giggles collide,
Mermaids echoing with joy and pride.
We dance like fools in the evening glow,
With every wave, our spirits flow.

So here we are at water's end,
With seaside tales that never bend.
The call of laughter, the sea's sweet tease,
In the warmth of dusk, we find our ease.

A Canvas of Sunrise and Salt

The sun swings low, what a sight,
Seagulls gossip, taking flight.
Coffee spills in a splashy dance,
While my breakfast plays its prance.

Canvas bright with color and cheer,
Fish in bow ties, pulling near.
Jellyfish in a conga line,
Who knew the ocean could be so fine?

Flip-flops flapping on the shore,
Chasing crabs who want to score.
My hat flies off, oh what a chase,
Waves giggle, leaving their trace.

Sunset plans, a beachy fuss,
Who brought snacks? Oh, it's a plus!
Dancing with shadows, without a care,
We laugh 'til twilight fills the air.

Notes from a Sailor's Heart

A sailor with a paper hat,
Writes love notes to the sea and brat.
His pencil's wet, the ink's a mess,
But the dolphins cheer, they're quite impressed.

Waves take turns, they throw a tease,
His compass spins, such mischief it sees.
A shrimp in boots gives a hearty nod,
As the sailor's jokes land like a clod.

Rusty anchor, oh what a find,
He claims it was a treasure, oh so blind!
The jellybean fish all roll their eyes,
While breezes snicker, it's quite the surprise.

So he sails on, with heart so free,
To a place where nonsense can just be.
His notes may flutter, his heart may race,
In the joy of waves, he finds his place.

Beyond the Surf's Embrace

Beyond the waves, a world so wild,
A crab with style acts like a child.
Splashing through puddles, oh what a thrill,
While fish gossip loudly, against their will.

Flip-flop fights, oh what a show,
Laughter erupts when someone lets go.
Mermaids giggle, sipping on foam,
Building sandcastles, converting them to home.

The seafoam dances a little jig,
While sea turtles argue who's the big wig.
Beach balls collide, in a colorful spree,
As pineapples roll away, naughty and free.

With each sunrise, a fresh new jest,
In this world of wide-eyed quest.
So bring your laughter, your heart so bright,
For the shores of joy, hold pure delight.

The Stillness of a Starlit Cove

Under a cloak of shimmering night,
Crickets sing while the moon shines bright.
Starfish dance with a wiggle and glee,
Oh, what a night! Just let it be.

In the silence, I hear a crack,
It's just my flip-flop, going off track.
The tides chuckle at my silly plight,
As shadows sway and embrace the light.

Campfire crackles, marshmallows fly,
S'mores get gobbled, oh my, oh my!
The ocean hums a lullaby tune,
With a wink from the bright, watchful moon.

So here we sit, friends close at hand,
Braving the night, so silly and grand.
In this cove, laughter twirls in the air,
Wrapped in the magic, we simply share.

The Harmony of Water and Light

The sun dips low, a sight so grand,
While crabs dance sideways on the sand.
Fish flip-flop, with styles unique,
While surfers fall, and it's quite the leak.

Seashells gossip with the tide's soft song,
Whispers of laughter where we all belong.
A seagull squawks, but no one cares,
For sandcastles rise in our playful lairs.

The piña colada flows like laughter,
While beach balls fly, the joy thereafter.
As waves crash down like a comic spree,
Nature's punchline is wild and free!

The ocean sparkles with a cheeky grin,
As jellyfish waltz, they sway and spin.
With every splash, we all agree,
Life's a joke, and we're the comedy!

Chronicles of the Coastal Breeze.

A flip-flop saga on the sandy shore,
With seagulls swooping, a feathery roar.
A toddler's tantrum, a runaway hat,
Even the crabs chuckle at that!

Beach towels tangled like tangled hair,
Looters of sunscreen in this sun-kissed lair.
The sand's so warm, it's like a hug,
But oh! Watch for the sneaky bug!

Kite-flying chaos, caught in a tree,
While the breeze laughs, oh so carefree.
A dolphin jumps, with a wink and spin,
In this magical realm where we all win!

It's lazy and crazy, this coastal life,
Just kick back, kick off the strife.
With coconut laughter shared by the sea,
Join in the fun, come laugh with me!

Whispers of the Island Wind

The wind whispers secrets, oh so sly,
As a toucan shouts, 'Look! I can fly!'
Mangoes drop like unexpected news,
While islanders swap their silly views.

The hammock sways with a giggling sigh,
While lizards dance, and we all comply.
A friendly pelican makes a face,
And the world feels like a comical place.

Underneath palms with a wink or cheer,
A coconut plops, and we all adhere.
On the porch where the laughter meets,
We toast to blunders with fruity treats.

As evening glows with a fiery light,
We tell tales bold, of silly flight.
With whispers carried on the blowing wind,
Life's a good joke, that won't rescind!

Dance of the Coconut Palms

Coconuts wobble, a dance that's sweet,
While monkeys swing with the nimblest feet.
A frisbee flies, the dog in hot chase,
As laughter erupts, can't keep a straight face.

Palm trees sway, with a rhythm divine,
While sand between toes feels quite sublime.
An earthworm wiggles with humorous pride,
As beach lovers gossip, side by side.

Shells in the sun sparkle like bling,
A clam jumps out for a random fling.
With sunburned noses, we sit and we cheer,
In a goofy parade that we hold dear.

When the sun dips low, the colors ignite,
We dance with shadows in the dimming light.
All through the evening, we share a good rhyme,
In this frolicsome place, we beat time!

Unwinding the Threads of Libations

Sipping coconuts on the sand,
With straw hats that don't quite stand.
The drink spills out, a slippery mess,
We laugh and joke, oh what a stress!

Seagulls join in, they squawk with glee,
Dancing around like they own the sea.
While chasing our snacks with flapping flair,
A beachside feast we hardly share!

With every sip, our giggles grow,
As the tide pulls back with a cheeky show.
Floating worries on waves that glide,
Let's belly laugh, and take a ride!

At sunset, we toast with silly cheers,
To the sun and waves, and our silly fears.
With every clink, mischief shines,
Unwinding all of life's old lines!

Echoing Laughter Beneath the Palms

Gathered 'neath the leafy shade,
With friends so wild, we're unafraid.
Our laughter bounces off the trees,
While admiring the dimples of the bees.

A coconut falls, it's a bit deranged,
We duck and dive, feeling quite strange.
Yet still we giggle, who would have thought,
That nature's antics would leave us caught?

With flip-flops flying, we race around,
Jumping over shells, thinking we're crowned.
The sun sets low, it's quite the scene,
As we crown ourselves with leaves so green!

So here's a toast to the days we've spun,
With friends and fun, and the warm sun.
May laughter echo, and never cease,
Under the palms where we find our peace!

Sea Turtles and Starlit Paths

A turtle stumbles, oh what a sight,
With flippers flapping, it's quite the flight.
We cheer it on with silly chants,
While hoping it joins our beachfront dance!

Moonlight sparkles on waves so wide,
As we join in with the tide's wild ride.
Wiggling our toes in the salty foam,
We make the shore our wacky home.

"Get your shells!" I shout with glee,
While dodging splashes from the squishy sea.
With starfish winks and playful swirls,
We let our laughter rock the world!

So spin those turtles, let them glide,
We're all just fish without a tide.
In this bustling sea of dreams we craft,
Embracing our laughter in a happy draft!

The Dance of the Sailor's Shadow

A sailor's shadow sways on deck,
With two left feet, what a funny wreck!
He spins and twirls, his hat goes flying,
As we all laugh, we start trying!

Up and down like a boat in sway,
His moves are wild, they're here to stay.
We cheer him on with raucous calls,
As he marches bravely and nearly falls!

His shadow dances with such delight,
On the shiny waves in the fading light.
With every stumble, we laugh until,
The sailor's shadow gives us a thrill!

Let's raise a toast to moments brief,
Full of laughter, joy, and silly relief.
For in this dance, we find our peace,
And sailing shadows that never cease!

Reflections in a Seafoam Mirror

A crab in a tux, looking so fine,
Struts on the beach, claiming it's time.
Seagulls are laughing, what a parade,
Chasing the tide, they're never afraid.

A fish in the surf, wearing a hat,
Swims with style, while dodging a cat.
The waves giggle softly, giving a cheer,
As sunbathers dance, sipping cold beer.

The starfish, a diva, on the dry sand,
Waves at the tourists, softening their tan.
With puns in the air, the ocean's delight,
Each splash tells a joke, from morning till night.

So let's raise our toes, in foam and in glee,
Join this mad circus, just you and me.
As laughter goes rolling, on waves shining bright,
In this silly lagoon, we'll frolic till night.

Sails Upon the Wind's Whisper

A parrot with shades, he squawks out a tune,
Steering the ship, beneath the big moon.
The captain is napping, dreams of a feast,
While fish throw a party, a seafood feast.

With sails full of giggles, we rise with the breeze,
A dolphin wears shorts, it's all about ease.
The compass spins round, lost in all fun,
While jellyfish jiggle, under the sun.

The crew sings in harmony, off-key and loud,
As they dive for the snacks, feeling so proud.
Bananas on deck, they slip and they slide,
Making each wave a gooey joyride.

In this salty adventure, we dance and we sway,
Chasing our troubles, they vanish away.
With winds of laughter, we'll sail 'til we drop,
This goofy escapade, we never will stop.

Cascades of Tropic Blooms

A flower named Daisy, in a bright yellow hat,
Claims she is queen, while flirting with a cat.
The sunflowers giggle, all swaying in tune,
As bees buzz around, dancing to a tune.

Stumbling through petals, a bear with a grin,
Trips on a tulip, but laughs goes in.
The daisies are blushing, their backs full of cheer,
As they spread wild stories, far and near.

The breeze carries whispers, jokes wrapped in light,
A coconut falls, what a comical sight!
Laughter erupts from this colorful patch,
As squirrels throw confetti, with a cheerful scratch.

In every bright bloom, a giggle is found,
Dancing with flowers, we twirl all around.
With petals and giggles, let's frolic and bloom,
In this carnival garden, there's always room.

Journeys Through the Celestial Blue

Like a fish on a bike, our dreams take a ride,
Making waves in the sky, with a whale as our guide.
The clouds all wave back, with puffs soft and white,
As we laugh through the heavens, in pure delight.

With a parrot navigator, all hoot and all yell,
We sail through the sunbeams, casting our spell.
Catching rainbows and giggles, we zoom through the air,
While clouds become pillows, our worries laid bare.

A seagull on roller skates zips past in a flash,
Leaving behind a trail of a wonderful splash.
The sun throws confetti, bright hues in the stream,
As we drift on this journey, wrapped up in a dream.

So let's chase the horizon, where laughter is free,
On this whimsical voyage, just you and me.
With each silly moment, we'll dance through the blue,
For there's joy in the journey, waiting for you.

Whispers of Ocean Winds

Seagulls squawk with silly flair,
As the salty air dances in hair.
Kites fly high, they twist and dive,
While flip-flops squish where crabs arrive.

A coconut falls, it lands with a thud,
Chasing a dog who slips in the mud.
Surfboards wait, but folks prefer
To nap in shade, as waves just purr.

Children squeal while building their sand,
With castles that never quite seem to stand.
The ocean laughs and teases their pride,
As water washes the towers aside.

So let your worries float far away,
In a sun-soaked land where we all play.
With every gust and each playful sound,
Joy comes whispering all around.

Dance of the Saltwater Waves

Waves tap-dance on the golden shore,
As clumsy crabs march, wanting more.
Surfboards wobble, then they glide,
While dolphins giggle, with playful pride.

Starfish throw their arms out wide,
While fish in schools do side-by-side.
Every splash is a silly cheer,
Echoes of laughter in the blue sphere.

Shells sparkle bright beneath the sun,
As tourists pose, thinking it's fun.
With ice cream cones, they run and leap,
While sticky hands make memories to keep.

The sun bows down, the night comes slow,
With fireflies dancing, putting on a show.
We'll sway to tunes from the nearby band,
As waves keep dancing on the soft sand.

Serenity in Sunlit Palms

Beneath the palms, we let out a sigh,
As a wayward kite soars high in the sky.
A squirrel steals snacks, with cheery delight,
While sunburned tourists glow in the light.

Bamboo drinks, with straws all askew,
Often spill over, not just a few.
Laughter erupts; it's a joyful mess,
As umbrellas tilt in a breezy caress.

A hammock sways, it's a game of fate,
As someone jumps in, it rotates!
The beach ball bounces, dodging the crowd,
While the sun smiles down, sunny and proud.

At dusk we share tales, with giggles and grins,
With the salt in our hair, and laughter that wins.
So let's toast to days where the fun never stops,
In this silly place where the joy always pops.

Echoes of the Island Song

Coconuts drop with a thundering crash,
As people jump up with a panicked dash.
Flip-flops fly, in a frantic dance,
While gulls laugh loud, at the silly prance.

A beach bonfire, the perfect heat,
But someone's marshmallows are stuck to their feet.
As we sing along with the island band,
One friend trips, and the laughter is grand.

With a sunset that paints the world anew,
Our shadows wave 'bye, as fun bids adieu.
Yet memories linger like waves on the shore,
And stories return, begging for more.

So here's to the moments where joy runs wild,
Where grown-ups act silly, like wide-eyed child.
In echoes of laughter from night until dawn,
The music of life keeps humming along.

Mirrors of the Infinite Deep

Reflections dance on the water's face,
Fish wear sunglasses, channeling grace.
Jellyfish juggling in a comical way,
While crabs play poker and clap for their pay.

Seagulls squawk jokes as they swoop by,
Stealing sandwiches from the beach-goers nearby.
A dolphin winks, flipping a wave,
While a turtle tells tales, oh so brave!

Bubbles burst with laughter, not a care,
As pelicans strut like they're on a dare.
In this watery world, all troubles cease,
Life's a party beneath the surface, at least!

So raise your drink with a splash and cheer,
For the funny friends that swim ever near.
With a flip and a flop, joy takes the stage,
As we all join in on this whimsical page.

Salt and Sunshine Whispers

The sun throws confetti through the leaves,
While crabs have decided to form their own leagues.
Fish in bow ties dance with flair,
While seaweeds gossip, floating with care.

A clam's got stories that make you grin,
As starfish twirl like they're ready to win.
The tide teases toes, gives a gentle tickle,
And a sea cucumber plays on with a giggle.

Seashells compete for the title of 'loud',
While the waves applaud, oh so proud.
A seagull strolls with a strut so bold,
Screaming the headlines of fish tales untold.

So bask in the laughter, soak up the fun,
As laughter flows wild beneath the hot sun.
With a splash and a cheer, let's never forget,
These salt-laden moments, the best lifebuoy yet!

A Voyage Amongst Sea Mist

Sailboats dance on the shimmering waves,
The captain's a monkey, howling bravely he saves.
Parrots perch with their colors so bright,
Trading tales of treasure, quite a sight!

The hull creaks softly, singing its tune,
While fish in the wake are a lively cartoon.
Mermaids in sunglasses exchange funny quips,
As they splash about with mischievous flips.

The compass spins, but none seem to care,
Because finding the laughter is the treasure we share.
As the mist wraps the world in a giggly haze,
Every wave brings a wink, a chuckle, a phrase.

So let's chart a course where the jokes come alive,
For on this wild journey, we all shall thrive.
With magic and mischief, let hearts set sail,
In this merry adventure, we'll always prevail!

Celestial Canopy Over Turquoise

Stars twinkle down, drizzling light so sweet,
While sea urchins dance to a sunken beat.
The moon's got jokes that the tides can't keep,
As waves giggle softly, lulling us to sleep.

A crab moonwalks under the midnight sky,
With a conch shell microphone, it's a star-studded hi.
The currents swirl secrets, tickling the night,
As rascally puffers puff up with delight.

Water glistens under constellations' embrace,
Where narwhals recount tales of a dangerous race.
A slippery eel in a tuxedo so neat,
Shows off its moves with a wink and a beat.

So dance in the shimmer, twirl in the glow,
For this watery world has a fun-filled show.
With laughter like bubbles rising with glee,
We'll sail through the night, wild and free!

Swaying Grass and Sundrenched Eyes

In a field where grass does sway,
Laughter dances every day.
With sun-kissed cheeks and silly grins,
We tumble down, the joy begins.

The ants march by in straight, neat lines,
While we eat snacks and share our signs.
A seagull swoops to steal a fry,
Then flaps away with a cheeky cry.

The sunbeams bounce from head to toe,
We plunge in pools with quite the show.
The splash is loud—oh! What a scene!
Who knew a dive could be so keen?

So let's embrace this light and cheer,
With giggles ringing, far and near.
Life is a joke, the punchline sweet,
In grassy realms, we find our beat.

A Tapestry Woven with Sea Breeze

The sails are full when winds take flight,
We hope the sea won't start a fight.
A crab does dance with clumsy glee,
While we just laugh, lost in the spree.

With flip-flops on, we race the tide,
Skidding past with nothing to hide.
A fish leaps up, but misses space;
It flops and rolls—what a funny face!

Mismatched socks and sandy toes,
The ocean's splash, it surely knows.
Our hair's a mess, but spirits high,
We're beach comedians, oh my, oh my!

Each wave that crashes fuels our jest,
In salty laughter, we find our rest.
So come along, let's share the jest,
In woven tales, we're truly blessed.

Chasing Stars on the Silken Water

At dusk we chase the sparkling lights,
Reflections dance on tranquil sights.
With nets and jars, we catch our dreams,
But only get wet—it's not as it seems.

The stars above begin to glow,
A fish pops up—oh, don't you know?
We grunt and sigh with playful woes,
As it evades our careful throws.

The gentle waves with whispers sweet,
Tug at our hearts in rhythmic beat.
Yet with our luck, the fish just laughs,
And swims away while we take halfs.

So let us spin and twirl in glee,
In chase of stars, so wild and free.
For laughter lingers, as it departs,
With catchy dreams and silly hearts.

The Secrets in the Ocean's Whisper

Beneath the waves, they giggle low,
Secrets drift like bubble blows.
A turtle grins and winks with glee,
While seaweed tickles, oh can't you see?

We dive for pearls and strange old shoes,
Find treasures lost that we gladly choose.
A crab gives chase, it's quite the scene,
As we trip over our own routine.

The ocean churns with tales to share,
While fish parade without a care.
We laugh so hard, we snort and squeak,
Mixing joy with salty cheek to cheek.

So listen close, the waves will say,
Life is odd in every way.
With secrets sewn in foam and spray,
We'll always find a reason to play.

The Caress of Warm Currents

A gull stole my sandwich, how rude!
I chased it down, feeling quite crude.
   But it laughed as it flew so high,
   While I blinked up, asking why.

The sun's a giant cheese in the sky,
As my skin turns red, oh my, oh my!
Seagulls chuckle, the jellyfish dance,
I'll join the fun, and take a chance.

Sandy toes and a playful grin,
Who knew the tide could be so thin?
   I fell into wave after wave,
   Like a fish, I misbehave!

And when the sunset turns to fire,
I'll bounce around, never tire.
With laughter echoing, the night begins,
As the ocean sings of my silly sins.

Ocean's Kiss in Evening Glow

The waves whisper secrets of fishy tricks,
As I dance 'round with sunburnt licks.
My hat flew off, taken by chance,
I yelled, 'Come back!', in a lack of stance.

Palms high-fived as I spilled my drink,
Sipping saltwater — oh, what do you think?
The crabs hold a party, I'm on the list,
Join us, they wave, you can't resist!

Each wave that crashes is a new surprise,
Like a clown with a wig and two googly eyes.
I surf the foam, but not with skill,
Flipping and flopping gives quite the thrill.

When the day's curtain starts to fall,
I'll serenade with a crabby call.
Under the stars, we laugh and glow,
A whimsical night, what a show!

Rhythms of the Shoreline Heartbeat

Footprints leading, then washed away,
I dance and prance on this bright ballet.
The sand, a mix of giggles and grains,
While I trip over my own two chains!

The tide and I — a goofy pair,
As it tickles my ankles without a care.
A coconut rolls straight into my leg,
I pick it up, ready to beg.

A starfish winked, or did I dream?
He surely chuckled at my ice cream.
With each splash, I call it a win,
Who needs luck when I have fin?

The sunset flaunts hues of orange and pink,
I take a bow, as I start to sink.
In laughter with waves, spirits will spark,
Let's celebrate this quirky arc!

Canvas of Dunes and Dusk

The sandcastles lean like tipsy towers,
Claiming they'll last for hours and hours.
I built a moat, but lo, it's gone,
The tide just laughed and said, 'Come on!'

Buried neck-deep, with only my head,
I giggle at crabs that summon dread.
A seagull's snicker floats through the air,
While I wave back, caught in a stare.

With kites in the sky, all colors afloat,
I tangle the strings, 'Oh, what a coat!'
The sun dips low, like a sleepy cat,
I plop on the dunes, s'what's so fat!

As twilight arrives with stars on parade,
I join the soft whispers, a funny charade.
In this silly realm, where the sun goes to rest,
The canvas unfolds, and I am blessed!

Journey through Aquatic Dreams

In a boat that's made of cheese,
Sailing past those fish with ease,
Dolphins jump, wave their fins,
Who knew they wore such silly grins?

Seagulls squawk in suits so bright,
Chasing shadows in the light,
Mermaids laugh with shells as hats,
Playing tag with funky cats!

Crabs in shades stroll side by side,
While starfish dance in ocean tide,
A turtle thinks he's quite a star,
But he's just driving a clunky car!

As waves crash down like a big parade,
My flip-flops fly, I'm quite afraid!
Yet laughter carries on the breeze,
Turned fish-slapped, I feel so at ease.

Mornings Wrapped in Seafoam

Waking up to jellyfish jam,
Toast is swimming, oh what a scam!
Sunshine spills on the breakfast plate,
My cereal's now going on a date!

Seashells giggle, waving good day,
While crabs compete in the sand ballet,
A pelican steals my bacon slice,
I chase him down – not very nice!

Sandcastles made of whipped cream sky,
I built one tall, but it said goodbye,
A wave came in with a cheeky grin,
Now my castle's wearing a fishy skin!

With flip-flop footprints on the sand,
I dance around, it's quite unplanned,
Laughter echoes with every sway,
Morning magic, come what may!

Dances of the Celestial Sea

Stars are twinkling on a wave,
A marlin's dancing, what a brave!
Octopus joins in with six left feet,
Their moves, my dear, they can't be beat!

Underneath the waves they prance,
Clownfish laughing in a trance,
Bubble-blowers get carried away,
While shrimp are having a salad buffet!

The moon's a disco ball tonight,
Even planktons are feeling light,
Jellyfish float, they're dressed to impress,
With LED lights, they're truly a mess!

Each wave a party, curl and crash,
Dancing dolphins in a flash,
Underwater, there's no contest,
In the sea, fun is a guest!

Emblems of Island Time

On a beach where coconuts sway,
I'm stuck in flip-flops on parade,
Sandy toes and goofy hats,
Wishing I could dance with the cats!

Pelicans pull pranks on all,
Diving down like a silly ball,
And here I sip my fruity drink,
As waves crash down, I laugh and wink!

Seashells whisper tales of yore,
Of pirate ships and treasure lore,
But here I am with ice cream stains,
Living large with silly gains!

Island time is a real delight,
Sun holds court from morning to night,
Laughing freely, we've lost our sense,
Letting joy be the greatest expense!

A Symphony of Sapphire Waves

Blue waves dance like wild gnomes,
Splashing joy in bubbly foams.
Seagulls laugh at clumsy dives,
While fish sing songs of silly jives.

A pirate's hat floats on its own,
Chasing dreams in a sea of foam.
Sunburned toes wiggle with glee,
The ocean's tickle, a funny spree.

Mermaids giggle behind the rocks,
Tickling crabs with tiny socks.
The rhythm of splashes, quite a treat,
As dolphins strut on their flippered feet.

Under the sun, where worries cease,
We dance like wobbly jellyfish with ease.
A symphony plays of splashes and cheer,
Ocean's humor shining, oh-so-clear!

Refuge in the Sunlit Coves

In cozy nooks where shadows play,
We sip on coconuts all day.
Sunburnt noses and silly hats,
Laughing at sunbathing chubby cats.

The tide rolls in like a playful pup,
Chasing sandcastles, let's scoop it up!
With salty snacks stuck on our lips,
We giggle as seaweed hugs our hips.

Butterflies dance in the ocean breeze,
Winking at tourists, aiming to please.
Swimmers flop like fish on land,
Trying to run, it's not well-planned.

Wave after wave, the laughter flows,
In this cove, anything goes.
Sunshine wraps our hearts so tight,
Making memories with every light!

Embrace of Ocean's Breath

Waves whistle tunes both loud and sweet,
Tickling toes and pounding feet.
Gulls squawk jokes from high above,
In this salty realm, there's so much love.

The ocean exhales with a laugh so bright,
As flip-flops joust in a bumbling fight.
A beach ball bounces like a hyper frog,
While people trip over a lazy dog.

Sun hats fly like runaway kites,
Chasing sandwiches on seaside nights.
In this embrace, chuckles unfold,
As treasure maps lead to a tub of gold!

Spraying water paints our cheeks,
In fits of giggles, we chase the peaks.
Each wave a tickle, each splash a grin,
In this hilarious place, let's dive right in!

Driftwood Dreams Under Starlit Skies

Driftwood tells tales of ocean lore,
While starlit skies sing 'nevermore.'
A clunky crab plays the magician,
As flip-flops dance, what a condition!

We build our castles out of sea snacks,
As the moon laughs at our silly hacks.
The tide rolls in to steal our fries,
While sea turtles wear funny ties.

Under the stars, we share our dreams,
With giggles galore and ice cream streams.
The whole beach bounces with merriment,
In driftwood tales, we find content.

As night closes with a shimmery wink,
We ponder life over a fizzy drink.
With laughter echoing in salty air,
These are the moments we love to share!

Glimpse of Paradise in Every Wave

In the sun, the seagulls dance,
Flip-flops squeak, what a chance!
Sandcastles rise, then quickly fall,
Time for ice cream, a sticky sprawl.

Waves are giggling, giving chase,
Water splashes, oh, the place!
A crab scuttles, with great finesse,
Lost my towel? Oh, what a mess!

Beach balls bounce in sunbeam play,
Surfboards tipping, come what may.
The lifeguard snoozes, dreams of fame,
Not a soul to blame but the waves' game.

Laughing kids, a playful fuss,
Find the treasure, what's the fuss?
In this spot, so joyous we stay,
Life's a beach, hip-hip-hooray!

The Journey of the Wandering Shore

Sandy feet, oh where to roam?
The shoreline calls, it feels like home.
With every step, a treasure's found,
A flip-flop's fate, stuck in the ground.

Seashells laughing, can you hear?
Whispers of jellyfish, oh dear!
A fishing hat flies up with glee,
Sorry, that one won't catch a pea!

Cocktail umbrellas in full swing,
An outing here is always king.
Finding crabs in a sunlit race,
No quicker critter in this place!

Seagulls squawk, what's on the menu?
Beach snacks, fish sticks for a venue.
As the tide rolls in, so does our cheer,
The wandering shore, we hold so dear!

A Treetop's Folly in the Breeze

Up in the palms, oh what a view,
Swinging like monkeys, here's what we do!
Coconut hats, how clever they seem,
A pirate's life? Just a silly dream.

Breezy whispers through leaves so green,
Swaying to rhythms, an unseen scene.
Lost my way to the coconut snack,
But found a parrot, oh what a quack!

Sunlight flickers, a dance of glee,
What's more fun than lunch on a tree?
But as I bite, it tumbles down,
Life's like fruit, you wear a crown!

Laughter mingles with rustling leaves,
Silly echoes, as mischief achieves.
In the hammock, a cozy plea,
This high-up world, just let it be!

Memories Written in Seashells

In the sand, our tales unfold,
Seashell secrets, stories bold.
A conch tells jokes, it truly does,
Crabs roll their eyes—oh, what a buzz!

Tidbits of laughter, mixed with sun,
Fossilized moments, oh, what fun!
The tide retreats with a splashing giggle,
Shells dance around in a happy wiggle.

Messages carved in a starfish's heart,
Sunset crayons, a colorful art.
Waves come rushing, trying to peek,
Shells whisper soft, no need to speak.

Memories made by the ocean's hand,
Silly moments upon the sand.
To cherish each shell, with joy we bring,
The memories of laughter—let's dance and sing!

www.ingramcontent.com/pod-product-compliance
Lightning Source LLC
Chambersburg PA
CBHW072221070526
44585CB00015B/1431